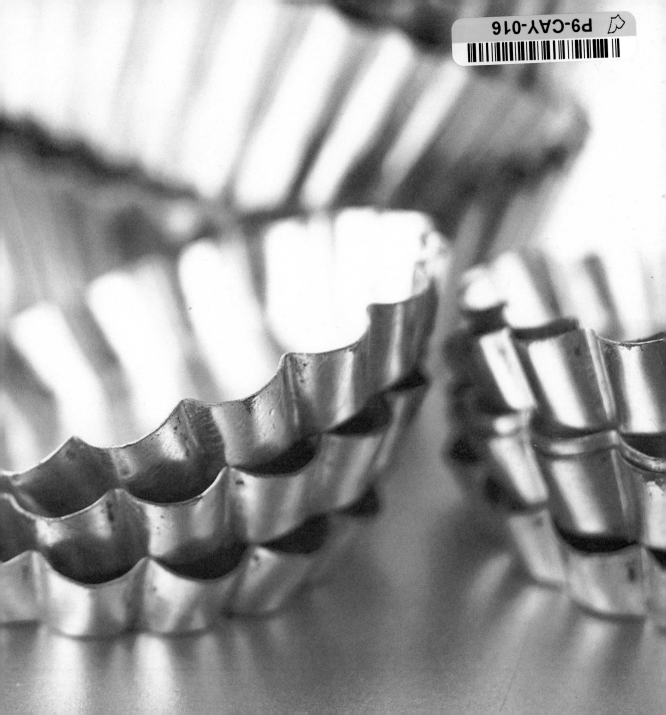

TEATIME

TEATIME

30 irresistible and delicious afternoon treats

Clare Gordon-Smith *with photography by* Philip Webb

TIME
LIFE
BOOKS

Alexandria, Virginia

TIME® LIFE BOOKS

Time-Life Books is a division of Time Life Inc.

TIME LIFE INC.
President and CEO: Jim Nelson

TIME-LIFE TRADE PUBLISHING
Vice President and Publisher   Neil Levin
Senior Director of Acquisitions
    and Editorial Resources   Jennifer Pearce
Director of New Product Development   Carolyn Clark
Director of Trade Sales   Dana Coleman
Director of Marketing   Inger Forland
Director of New Product Development   Teresa Graham
Director of Custom Publishing   John Lalor
Director of Special Markets   Robert Lombardi
Director of Creative Services   Laura McNeill
Project Manager   Jennie Halfant
Technical Specialist   Monika Lynde

Printed and bound in China by Toppan Printing Co.
10 9 8 7 6 5 4 3 2 1

TIME-LIFE is a trademark of Time Warner Inc., and affiliated companies.

Library of Congress Cataloging-in-Publication Data
Gordon-Smith, Clare
  Teatime : 30 irresistible and delicious afternoon treats / Clare Gordon-Smith
with photography by Philip Webb
    p. cm.
ISBN 0-7370-2036-9 (hardcover)
1. Afternoon teas. 2. Desserts. I. Title.
TX736 .G67 2000
641.5'3–dc21   99-040073

First published in the United Kingdom in 2000
by Ryland Peters & Small, Cavendish House, 51-55 Mortimer Street, London W1N 7TD

Books produced by Time-Life Trade Publishing are available at a special bulk discount for promotional
and premium use. Custom adaptions can also be created to meet your specific marketing goals.
Call 1-800-323-5255

Acknowledgments:
My thanks to Stephen Twining at Twinings, who showed me the whole tea process from Sri Lanka
to London; Charlotte Doherty at The Four Seasons Hotel, London; Pippa Watts at Jane Howard PR;
Rosemary Scoular at Peters Fraser & Dunlop. Thanks also to the team at Ryland Peters & Small and
Philip Webb and, as always, a big thank you to my family.

**Notes: Before baking, always weigh or measure all the necessary ingredients exactly and
prepare baking pans or sheets. Ovens should be preheated to the specified temperature. If
using a fan-assisted oven, adjust cooking times according to the manufacturer's instructions.**

setting the scene

Teatime—when tea is served with delicious sandwiches, scones, cakes, and pastries—is one of my favorite times of the day. It is a custom that has evolved gradually over time, but is associated mainly with the British. In eighteenth-century London, society ladies would satisfy their hunger for refreshments and gossip between lunch and dinner. Then later, in the 1800s teashops and coffeeshops became popular venues for social gatherings.

Since the 1950s a faster pace of life and a change in family structure have resulted in the demise of this everyday ritual. It has been relegated to more relaxed gatherings, usually at the weekend. Modern teatime has also ventured out of the drawing room and into the boardroom, joining the fashionable trend for breakfast meetings and working lunches.

A traditional afternoon tea should be served in style: on a crisp, white, linen-covered table, with fine bone china teacups and teaplates, delicate silverware and a cake stand. But for a less formal occasion, you can use whatever tableware you want. It is also fun to take teatime outdoors, weather permitting.

Everyone has their favorite teatime treat, be it fruitcake, gingerbread, or scones with whipped heavy cream and strawberry jam. Include a selection of sweet and savory dishes at teatime—and plenty of freshly brewed tea.

choosing tea

Of the dozens of different tea styles available, which are best for afternoon tea? There are three basic kinds of tea; black, green, or oolong.

Black teas, a Western preference, are fermented before drying. They are rich, full-flavored, and aromatic and account for the largest sales in the tea market. Assam, from northeast India, is a popular black tea, with a strong malty flavor. Darjeeling, the champagne of teas, makes an aromatic, red-orange brew. Ceylon, from Sri Lanka, is another black tea. It is mild with a mellow, nutty flavor, which complements both sweet and savory foods—perfect for afternoon tea. Less common, but fine nonetheless, is China Keemun, a Chinese black tea. It is delicately perfumed with a nutty, slightly sweet flavor. Also from China is China Yunnan. Grown in the country's remote southwest region, this black variety gives a golden tea with rounded flavor. Rose Pouchong is blended with rose petals for a scented bouquet. Other blended black teas include Lapsang Souchong—a connoisseur tea with a distinctive smoky flavor—and the bergamot-scented Earl Grey, made with China teas and sometimes Darjeeling.

Green teas, favored in the East, are unfermented—and closest to the natural leaf. They are cool, clean, and refreshing and primarily from China, Japan, and Taiwan. Always served without milk, green teas are usually drunk after dinner rather than at teatime. Top-grade green teas include Jasmine tea and Gunpowder Green.

Oolong teas, such as Formosa Oolong, are semi-fermented and highly prized. Many people believe they should be savored on their own.

For the tea connoisseur, the best tea will come unblended and from single tea estates.

opposite page:
Rose Pouchong—a black tea flavored with rose petals. Best drunk without milk.

this page, from left:
Jasmine—a green tea flavored with jasmine petals; China Oolong—high-quality, usually drunk without milk; Gunpowder Green—always drunk without milk.

the perfect cup of tea

Buy top-quality tea leaves and store in an airtight container to maintain freshness.

Fill the kettle with freshly drawn cold water and boil. Never reheat water, as it contains less oxygen and will give tea a stale taste.

Warm the teapot with hot water, then empty. This ensures that the boiling water is not cooled when it hits the tea leaves and encourages the leaves to open properly.

Allow one heaped teaspoon of tea leaves per person, plus one for the pot.

Brew don't stew. Steep green teas for about 3 minutes and black and oolong teas for up to 5 minutes. If you prefer a weaker tea, taste it after 2 minutes, then at 2-minute intervals until ready to drink. Stir before pouring.

Pour the tea into the cup through a strainer. Drink with or without milk, or lemon and sugar, depending on preference or tea variety.

Keep the teapot clean. A build up of tannin will spoil future brews, so thoroughly rinse the pot in hot water (without detergent) afterward. Never wash teapots in a dishwasher.

salmon open sandwiches
with *marinated cucumber and dill*

A fabulous Scandinavian-style sandwich. Rye bread—rich and dense—is a perfect contrast to the delicate flavor of salmon. Rye acts as a firm sandwich base, keeping the topping in place.

To make the marinated cucumber, start the day before serving. Finely slice the cucumber using a mandoline or sharp knife and put in a shallow dish. Drizzle with the vinegar, add the dill and sugar, then cover, and marinate overnight. Alternatively, if time is short, let the mixture stand for at least 10-15 minutes.

To assemble the open sandwiches, spread the rye bread lightly with butter, then cut into triangles. Trim the salmon, pile onto the bread, and top with the marinated cucumber.

Marinated cucumber:
1 cucumber, about 7 inches long
2 tablespoons white wine vinegar
2 tablespoons chopped fresh dill
a pinch of sugar

4 slices rye bread
unsalted butter, for spreading
5 oz. smoked salmon

Serves 4

bread cups
with *roasted tomatoes, pesto, and olives*

Slices of bread, molded then toasted, make marvelous containers for savory ingredients. Choose your favorite bread—I like an organic whole wheat or white farmhouse loaf.

36 small plum tomatoes

olive oil, for brushing

12 thick slices whole wheat bread, crusts removed

4 tablespoons melted butter or olive oil

¾ cup prepared pesto

12 black olives, pitted and halved

salt and freshly ground black pepper

a baking sheet

a 2½-inch fluted cookie cutter

a 12-cup shallow muffin pan

Serves 6

Preheat the oven to 400°F. Cut the tomatoes in half lengthwise and arrange on a baking sheet. Brush with a little olive oil and sprinkle with salt and black pepper. Roast for 15-20 minutes until soft and browned around the edges. Remove and set aside.

Roll out the bread with a rolling pin until thin, then stamp out rounds with the cookie cutter. Line the muffin pan with the bread discs, pressing them firmly into the holes. Brush with the melted butter or oil and bake at the same temperature for about 7-10 minutes until crisp.

To serve, spoon the pesto into the bread cups, top with the roasted tomatoes and olives, and, if necessary, return to the oven for a few minutes to warm through.

egg and cress sandwiches

Teatime just isn't teatime without egg sandwiches—an all-time favorite. Here, I've used walnut bread as a delicious alternative to the classic white variety.

2 eggs

2 tablespoons mayonnaise

1 tablespoon crème fraîche or sour cream

unsalted butter, for spreading

8 slices walnut bread

a handful of watercress or arugula, tough stalks removed

salt and freshly ground black pepper

Serves 4

Put the eggs in a saucepan of cold water and bring to a boil. Reduce the heat and simmer for 5-6 minutes, then drain immediately and cool under cold running water. Peel the eggs when cold.

Coarsely chop the eggs and put them in a bowl with the mayonnaise, crème fraîche or sour cream, salt, and pepper. Mix well.

To assemble the sandwiches, spread the bread lightly with butter and divide the egg mixture between 4 of the slices. Add the watercress or arugula and top with the remaining bread.

brioche
with *prosciutto, pear, and parsley*

Juicy, sweet pears bring out the rich flavor of prosciutto—
a modern version of the traditional ham sandwich.

To make the parsley butter, put the ingredients in a bowl and mix. Spread the slices of brioche or challah with a thin layer of the herb butter. Top with a fold of prosciutto, pear slices, and strawberry pieces, if using. Add a leaf of parsley to each one, then serve.

4 slices of brioche or challah

4 slices prosciutto

1 ripe pear, cored and sliced lengthwise

1 strawberry, quartered (optional)

flat-leaf parsley, to serve

Parsley butter:

4 tablespoons unsalted butter, softened

1 tablespoon chopped parsley

Serves 4

mini carrot polenta muffins
with *herbed cream cheese*

Take teatime outdoors in the summer for a tea party in the sun. These muffins travel well, so pack them for a picnic and don't forget to take a thermos of tea and a blanket to sit on.

Preheat the oven to 400°F. Sift the flour and baking powder into a large bowl, then stir in the cornmeal and cayenne pepper. In another bowl, mix the milk with the butter and eggs. Add to the dry ingredients, stirring quickly with a wooden spoon until just mixed. Add the grated carrots, orange zest and juice, then mix quickly to make a coarse, slightly streaky batter. Do not beat or overmix.

Spoon the mixture into the prepared muffin pans and bake for about 12-15 minutes until just firm and golden. Let cool in the pans for about 1 minute, then turn out onto a wire rack to cool completely.

To make the herbed cream cheese, beat all the ingredients together until light and fluffy. To serve, split the muffins and fill with the herbed cheese.

2⅔ cup all-purpose flour

3 teaspoons baking powder

⅓ cup cornmeal

a pinch of cayenne pepper

⅔ cup milk

5½ tablespoons unsalted butter, melted

2 eggs, lightly beaten

5 oz. carrots, peeled and grated

grated zest and juice of 1 orange

Herbed cream cheese:

1 cup cream cheese

2 tablespoons snipped chives

1 tablespoon chopped parsley

three 12-cup deep mini muffin pans,
  lightly greased

Makes 36

sun-dried tomato scones

Capture the essence of Italy with sun-dried tomatoes. For extra pizzazz, eat the scones with an herb butter (page 61).

Preheat the oven to 400°F. Sift the flour, baking powder, salt, and cayenne pepper into a large bowl. Rub in the cubes of butter with your fingertips until the mixture looks like fine crumbs, then stir in the cheese and sun-dried tomatoes.

Gradually add the milk and mix to form a soft but not sticky dough. Turn out onto a lightly floured surface and pat out to about 1-inch thick. Dip the cookie cutter in flour and press out rounds. Gather the trimmings, pat out again, and cut out more rounds.

Put the scones well apart on the baking sheet and brush the tops with milk. Bake for 12–15 minutes until risen and golden. Remove from the oven. Serve warm or let cool on a wire rack. Eat with butter.

Variation:

Ham and Chive Scones: Omit the cayenne pepper and sun-dried tomatoes. Add ¼ cup chopped ham and 1 tablespoon snipped chives to the rubbed-in flour mixture, then proceed with the recipe.

1¾ cups all-purpose flour, plus extra for dusting

3 teaspoons baking powder

a pinch of salt

¼ teaspoon cayenne pepper

4 tablespoons unsalted butter, chilled and cut into cubes

1 cup Cheshire cheese or cheddar cheese, grated

1 tablespoon sun-dried tomatoes, finely chopped

½ cup milk, plus extra for brushing

To serve:
unsalted butter, softened

a 2-inch plain cookie cutter
a baking sheet, lightly greased

Makes 12

vegetable salad sandwich

At The Four Seasons Hotel in London, afternoon tea is an occasion to savor as well as remember. This sandwich is based on one that I ate when I attended a meeting there.

To prepare the filling, finely chop the cucumber and scallions. Halve and seed the peppers, then cut into small pieces. Transfer the prepared vegetables to a bowl, add the mayonnaise, crème fraîche or sour cream, parsley, salt, and pepper. Mix well.

To assemble the sandwiches, spread the bread lightly with butter, divide the filling between 4 of the slices, and add the watercress, if using. Top with the remaining bread. Cut into triangles.

Variation:
Smoked Chicken Salad: Mix ¾ cup shredded, smoked chicken with the filling. If the mixture is too dry, add extra mayonnaise.

Filling:
½ cucumber, about 3½ inches
   long
2 scallions
½ red pepper
½ yellow pepper
2 tablespoons mayonnaise
1 tablespoon crème fraîche or sour cream
1 tablespoon finely chopped parsley
salt and freshly ground black pepper
a handful of watercress leaves (optional)

8 slices whole wheat bread,
   crusts removed
unsalted butter, for spreading

Serves 4-6

rhubarb galette

Thin, crisp pastry topped with strips of rose-pink rhubarb. Impressive yet easy to make, this teatime galette doubles as a dessert. Use apples or pears if rhubarb is out of season.

Preheat the oven to 400°F. Roll out the pastry into a 4 x 8 inch rectangle. Transfer to the baking sheet and chill for 10-15 minutes.

Put the sugar in a saucepan with ½ cup water. Gently heat until the sugar dissolves, then increase the heat and boil for 1 minute until syrupy. Add the rhubarb pieces and cook for about 5-7 minutes until tender.

Remove with a slotted spoon and arrange in a single layer on the pastry, leaving a ¼-inch edge of pastry uncovered. Discard the syrup. Bake for 15-20 minutes until puffed and golden. Remove from the oven.

Put the apricot jam in a saucepan with 1 tablespoon water. Heat until the mixture begins to bubble, then brush over the rhubarb. Let cool, then serve with whipped cream and a dusting of cinnamon, if using.

8 oz. frozen puff pastry, thawed
¼ cup sugar
1 lb. rhubarb, cut into 2-inch lengths
¼ cup apricot jam, to glaze

To serve:
whipped heavy cream
ground cinnamon (optional)

a nonstick baking sheet

Serves 4-6

strawberry and blueberry tart
with *mascarpone*

Make this tart with your favorite berries: strawberries and blueberries are perfect partners and look impressive too.

Preheat the oven to 400°F. Put the flour and butter in a bowl and rub together with your fingertips until the mixture looks like fine crumbs. Stir in the sugar and egg yolk, then add enough cold water to make a soft but not sticky dough. Knead briefly, then wrap and chill for about 10 minutes or until ready to use.

Roll out the pastry and use to line the tart pan. Prick the base with a fork and chill for 10–15 minutes. Bake for about 20 minutes until golden. Remove from the oven and let cool.

Mix the mascarpone with the cream, then spoon into the tart shell. Pile the strawberries and blueberries on top, then sprinkle with the sugar.

Pie-crust pastry:

2 cups all-purpose flour

8 tablespoons (1 stick) unsalted butter, chilled and cut into cubes

1 tablespoon sugar

1 egg yolk

Filling:

4 tablespoons mascarpone cheese

2 tablespoons whipped heavy cream

1½ cups strawberries, hulled and halved

1¾ cups blueberries

1 tablespoon sugar

an 8-inch deep tart pan

Serves 4–6

lemon tartlets

Used in a rich, creamy custard, the zing of fresh lemons makes delicious teatime tartlets or a filling for a large tart.

Preheat the oven to 375°F. Roll out the pastry to ¼-inch thick and use to line the tartlet tins. Prick with a fork, then chill for 10–15 minutes. Line each tartlet with parchment paper, fill with baking beans, and bake blind for 10 minutes. Remove the beans and paper, then bake uncovered for 5 minutes. Remove from the oven. Lower the oven temperature to 325°F.

To make the lemon filling, put all the ingredients in a heatproof bowl set over a saucepan of simmering water. Stir constantly until the mixture thickens and looks like thin custard, about 30 minutes. Pour into the part-cooked pastry shells and bake for 20 minutes until set. Remove from the oven and let cool.

To make the topping, put the sugar in a small saucepan with ½ cup water. Gently heat until the sugar dissolves, then increase the heat and boil for 1 minute until syrupy. Reduce the heat, add the lemon slices, and cook until tender, about 10–12 minutes. Drain them and use to decorate the tartlets. Let cool, then serve dusted with confectioners' sugar.

1 quantity pie-crust pastry (page 26)

Lemon filling:
finely grated zest and juice of 2 large lemons
¾ cup sugar
3 eggs, lightly beaten
⅔ cup heavy cream

Topping:
¼ cup sugar
2 lemons, thinly sliced
confectioners' sugar, for dusting

12 tartlet tins, 3-inch diameter

Makes 12

chocolate puffs

Cream-filled pastries are heavenly—so light and airy—and hard to resist. Based on the classic éclair, these puffs are bound to be popular with children as well as grown-ups.

Preheat the oven to 400°F. To make the choux paste, melt the butter in ½ cup water in a saucepan over low heat. Bring to a boil, remove from the heat, and tip in the flour all at once. Add the salt. Beat quickly with a wooden spoon until the mixture comes away from the sides of the pan to form a soft ball. Let cool for 2 minutes, then beat in the eggs, a little at a time, until the paste is smooth, glossy, and forms soft peaks. Spoon into a piping bag fitted with a ½-inch plain nozzle and pipe 1¼-inch lengths, spaced 2 inches apart on the prepared baking sheets.

Bake, one sheet at a time, until puffed and golden. Remove from the oven and pierce each puff to release steam. Cool on a wire rack. Slit open the puffs and fill with the whipped cream and berries.

Using a teaspoon, drizzle the melted chocolate over the filled puffs. Let set, then serve.

Choux paste:
4 tablespoons unsalted butter, cut into cubes
½ cup all-purpose flour, sifted
a pinch of salt
2 eggs, lightly beaten

Filling:
1 cup heavy cream, whipped
½ cup strawberries, hulled and cut into small pieces
½ cup blueberries

Topping:
4 oz. bittersweet chocolate, melted

two baking sheets, lightly greased

Makes 32

pear frangipane tartlets

Frangipane—a creamed almond filling for tarts, pastries, and cookies—was invented by Parisian pâtissiers in the sixteenth century. Serve these delicious tarts as the finale to teatime.

1 quantity pie-crust pastry (page 26)

4 small pears

juice of ½ lemon

¼ cup apricot jam, to glaze

Frangipane:

4 tablespoons unsalted butter, softened

⅔ cup sugar

2 eggs, lightly beaten

1⅔ cups ground almonds

¼ cup all-purpose flour, sifted

12 tartlet tins, 3-inch diameter

Makes 12

Preheat the oven to 400°F. Roll out the pastry to ¼-inch thick and use to line the tartlet tins. Prick the bases with a fork, then chill for 10-15 minutes.

Halve, core, and slice the pears lengthwise. Put them in a bowl with the lemon juice and toss well to coat (this will prevent them from browning).

To make the frangipane, put the butter and sugar in a bowl and cream until light and fluffy. Beat in the eggs, a little at a time, then fold in the ground almonds and flour. Spoon the mixture into the tartlet shells and top with the pear slices. Bake for 15-20 minutes until golden. Remove from the oven.

To glaze the tartlets, put the apricot jam in a saucepan with 1 tablespoon water. Heat until the mixture begins to bubble, then brush over the tartlets. Let cool, then serve.

spiced shortbread

A traditional teatime cookie from Scotland. You know when you have a fine shortbread: it is just golden, snaps crisply, has an intense butter flavor and a melt-in-the mouth crumb.

Preheat the oven to 350°F. Put the flour and apple-pie spice in a bowl. Rub in the butter with your fingertips until the mixture looks like fine crumbs. Add the sugar, stir to mix, then bring the mixture together to form a dough.

Turn out onto a floured surface, knead 2-3 times, then roll out to about ¼-inch thick. Using the cookie cutter, stamp out as many rounds as possible. Gather the trimmings, roll out again, and press out more rounds. Repeat until all the dough has been used.

Put the shortbread on the prepared baking sheets, prick with a fork, and bake for 10-15 minutes until just golden. Remove from the oven and transfer to a wire rack to cool. Lightly dust with confectioners' sugar.

1 cup all-purpose flour, sifted
a pinch of apple-pie spice
8 tablespoons (1 stick) unsalted
   butter
⅓ cup sugar
confectioners' sugar, for dusting

a 2-inch fluted cookie cutter
two baking sheets, lightly greased

Makes 18-20

coffee kisses

A cross between a cookie and a cake, these coffee kisses are sandwiched together with wonderful coffee buttercream.

Preheat the oven to 350°F. Using a wooden spoon or electric mixer, beat the butter and sugar until light and creamy. Mix in the egg yolk, coffee extract, and milk, then the flour and baking powder. The mixture should be firm.

Spoon 24 small heaps of the mixture onto the prepared baking sheets and bake for 15-20 minutes until lightly golden. Remove from the oven and transfer to a wire rack to cool.

To make the coffee buttercream, beat the butter, confectioners' sugar, and coffee extract in a bowl until light and fluffy. Sandwich pairs of coffee kisses together with the filling. Lightly dust with confectioners' sugar, then serve.

8 tablespoons (1 stick) unsalted butter, softened
⅓ cup sugar
1 egg yolk
2 teaspoons coffee extract
1 tablespoon milk
1¾ cups all-purpose flour, sifted
½ teaspoon baking powder

Coffee buttercream:
8 tablespoons (1 stick) unsalted butter, softened
1⅓ cups confectioners' sugar, sifted, plus extra for dusting
1 teaspoon coffee extract

two baking sheets, lightly greased

florentines

Jewellike and lacy, Florentines have a rich butterscotch flavor and soft, chewy texture. Despite an Italian-sounding name, Florentines are specialities from Germany and Austria.

Preheat the oven to 375°F. Put the butter and sugar in a large saucepan and heat until the butter melts and the sugar dissolves. Add the flour and cook, stirring, for 1 minute, then add the cream and stir until thickened. Add the almonds, mixed candied fruit, and candied cherries. Mix well.

Space 4 heaped teaspoons of the mixture well apart on the prepared baking sheets. Pat each mound flat with the back of a spoon. Bake, one sheet at a time, for 10-15 minutes until golden. Remove from the oven, let cool on the baking sheet for 1 minute, then transfer to a wire rack to cool completely. Repeat, cooking in batches, until all the mixture has been used.

Dip a teaspoon into the melted chocolate, and trail it backwards and forwards quickly over 2-3 Florentines. Repeat until all the Florentines have been decorated. Let set, then serve.

½ **cup plus 1 tablespoon unsalted butter**

½ **cup plus 2 tablespoons sugar**

3 **tablespoons all-purpose flour, sifted**

3 **tablespoons heavy cream**

1½ **cups flaked almonds**

⅓ **cup diced mixed candied fruit**

¼ **cup green, red and yellow candied cherries, coarsely chopped**

4 **oz. bittersweet chocolate, melted, to decorate**

two baking sheets, lined with waxed paper or parchment

Makes 20-24

chocolate raisin cookies

These easy-to-make chewy cookies are simply divine. Use plump California raisins for maximum flavor and texture.

Preheat the oven to 350°F. Using a wooden spoon or electric hand-mixer, beat the butter with the sugars until light and creamy. Gradually beat in the egg. Fold in the flour, baking powder, and baking soda. Coarsely chop the chocolate, then add to the cookie mixture with the raisins. Mix well.

Put heaped spoonfuls of the mixture, spaced apart, on the prepared baking sheets. Bake for about 15-20 minutes until golden. Remove from the oven and let cool on a wire rack.

8 tablespoons (1 stick) unsalted butter, softened

½ cup light brown sugar

¼ cup sugar

1 egg, lightly beaten

1⅓ cups all-purpose flour, sifted

½ teaspoon baking powder

¼ teaspoon baking soda

3 oz. semisweet chocolate

½ cup raisins

two baking sheets, greased

Makes 24-26

macaroons

You will love macaroons if, like me, you hanker for something sweet yet light at teatime. They have a crisp exterior that belies a soft, chewy interior—the contrast in texture is magical.

Preheat the oven to 325°F. Put the ground almonds, sugar, and rice flour in a bowl. Add the egg white and mix well.

Line the baking sheet with rice paper. Put heaped spoonfuls of the almond mixture, spaced apart, on the prepared baking sheet. Flatten slightly.

Press a whole almond on top of each macaroon, then bake for 20-25 mintues until just golden. Remove from the oven and let cool on a wire rack. Break off and discard the excess rice paper from around the edges of the macaroons.

1¼ cups ground almonds

½ cup sugar

1 teaspoon rice flour

1 large egg white

rice paper*

10–12 whole blanched almonds, to decorate

a baking sheet

Makes 10-12

*Note: Edible rice paper is available from specialty grocers and gourmet food stores.

fudge brownies

4 oz. bittersweet chocolate

8 tablespoons (1 stick) plus 1 teaspoon unsalted butter, softened

1 cup plus 1 tablespoon sugar

1 teaspoon pure vanilla extract

2 eggs, lightly beaten

¾ cup plus 2 tablespoons self-rising flour, sifted

½ teaspoon salt

1 cup pecans, coarsely chopped

an 8-inch square cake pan, greased and lined with waxed paper or parchment

Makes 9 squares

Everyone loves rich, chocolate brownies. You can't beat this classic cookie at teatime.

Preheat the oven to 350°F. Melt the chocolate in a bowl set over a pan of simmering water. (Don't let the water touch the bowl or let any steam or water come into contact with the chocolate.)

Put the butter and sugar in a bowl and, using a wooden spoon or electric hand-mixer, beat until creamy. Add the melted chocolate and vanilla extract and mix well. Gradually beat in the eggs. Add the flour and salt and stir gently to mix—do not beat or overmix. Fold in the pecans. Spoon the mixture into the prepared cake pan and bake for 35-40 minutes or until a toothpick inserted into the center comes out clean. Let cool in the pan and cut into 9 squares.

gingerbread

Ginger is one of the world's oldest and best-loved spices— it's what makes this cake so fabulous. For an irresistible, effect, let the frosting run down the sides of the cake.

Preheat the oven to 325°F. Put the flour, ground ginger, and baking soda in a bowl. Stir to mix, then make a well in the center. Add the molasses, oil, and brown sugar and mix well. (The mixture will be dry.) Gradually beat in the egg and milk to make a lump-free batter.

Pour the mixture into the prepared loaf pan and bake for about 1 hour until risen and a toothpick inserted into the center comes out clean. Remove from the oven and turn out onto a wire rack set over a tray. Let cool.

To make the glacé frosting, mix the lemon juice with the confectioners' sugar to form a thin paste. Put the chopped ginger on top of the gingerbread, then pour over the frosting, allowing it dribble down the sides of the cake. Let set until firm, then serve.

1⅓ cups all-purpose flour, sifted
1 tablespoon ground ginger
1 teaspoon baking soda
⅓ cup molasses
3½ tablespoons vegetable oil
⅓ cup dark brown sugar
1 egg, lightly beaten
½ cup milk

glacé frosting:
2 tablespoons lemon juice
⅓ cup confectioners' sugar, sifted
¼ cup crystallized ginger, chopped

an 8½ x 4½ x 2½ inch loaf pan,
  greased and lined with waxed
  paper or parchment

Serves 8

hazelnut roulade

The lightest and airiest of all sponge cakes, filled with crème fraîche and raspberries. Blueberries are great too.

Preheat the oven to 400°F. Put the eggs and sugar in a large bowl and, using an electric hand-mixer, whisk until pale, thick, and creamy. The mixture should leave a ribbonlike trail on the surface when lifted.

Using a large metal spoon, fold in the flour and hazelnuts. Drizzle the melted butter over the surface of the mixture, then fold it in carefully.

Pour the mixture into the prepared jelly roll pan and level the surface. Bake for 15-20 minutes until golden and the sponge springs back when lightly pressed.

Remove from the oven and turn out onto parchment paper sprinkled with sugar. Peel off the lining paper and trim the edges of the roulade. Roll up the sponge from the short end with the paper inside. Let cool.

When ready to fill, gently unroll the sponge and remove the paper. Spread with a layer of crème fraîche, add the raspberries, and roll up as before. Dust with confectioners' sugar, then slice, and serve.

6 eggs
¾ cup plus 1 tablespoon sugar, plus extra for sprinkling
¼ cup plus 1 tablespoon self-rising flour, sifted
½ cup hazelnuts, toasted and finely ground
1 tablespoon unsalted butter, melted
confectioners' sugar, for dusting

Filling:
¾ cup heavy cream, whipped
1 cup raspberries

a 12 x 8 x 1 inch jelly roll pan, greased and lined with waxed paper or parchment

Serves 6-8

rich fruitcake

Crammed full of fruit, nuts, and spices, for a cake rich in flavor and texture. No tea party is complete without one.

10 tablespoons unsalted butter, softened

¾ cup sugar

3 eggs, lightly beaten

1 cup all-purpose flour, sifted

½ teaspoon baking powder

½ teaspoon ground cinnamon

½ teaspoon ground ginger

1 cup mixed dried fruit, such as raisins, golden raisins, and currants

¼ cup candied cherries, chopped

¼ cup crystallized ginger, chopped

⅓ cup whole blanched almonds, chopped, plus extra for decoration

a 7-inch round cake pan, greased and lined with a double layer of waxed paper or parchment

Preheat the oven to 325°F. Put the butter and sugar in a large bowl and, using a wooden spoon or electric hand-mixer, beat until light and creamy. Gradually beat in the eggs, a little at a time, then fold in the flour, baking powder, cinnamon, and ground ginger. Fold in the remaining ingredients.

Spoon the mixture into the prepared pan and decorate with whole almonds. Bake for 1½–2 hours until golden and a toothpick inserted into the center comes out clean. Remove from the oven, let cool in the pan for about 30 minutes, then turn out onto to a wire rack to cool completely.

chocolate spice muffins

Sugar and spice and all things nice. A cornucopia of great flavors—rich chocolate, aromatic spice, and nutty syrup—merge to make an extra-special teatime treat.

Preheat the oven to 350°F. Melt the butter, sugar, and syrup in a saucepan over low heat. Stir in the milk and heat gently until lukewarm.

Sift the dry ingredients into a bowl and make a well in the center. Using a whisk or electric hand-mixer, gradually mix in the liquid to make a lump-free batter.

Spoon the mixture into the muffin cases, filling each to about three-quarters full. Bake for 20–25 minutes until firm. Remove from the oven and let cool on a wire rack.

To make the chocolate fudge frosting, heat the butter, sugar, and milk until melted. Sift the confectioners' sugar and cocoa into a bowl and pour in the melted butter mixture. Beat until smooth. Using a spatula, spread a little of the frosting over each muffin, swirling it into a peak. Let set until firm, then serve.

8 tablespoons (1 stick) unsalted butter

¾ cup sugar

1 cup maple syrup

1 cup milk

2 cups self-rising flour

⅓ cup unsweetened cocoa

1 teaspoon baking soda

a pinch of salt

a pinch of apple-pie spice

Chocolate fudge frosting:

2 tablespoons unsalted butter

⅓ cup dark brown sugar

¼ cup milk

1⅔ cups confectioners' sugar

½ cup unsweetened cocoa

two 12-cup deep muffin pans, lined with 18 muffin paper cases

Makes 18

madeleines

A pretty, scallop-shaped small cake, made famous by the writings of Marcel Proust—perfect for afternoon tea with other fancies such as Florentines and macaroons.

Preheat the oven to 375°F. Put the eggs, sugar, and lemon zest, if using, in a large bowl. Using an electric hand-mixer, whisk until pale, thick, and creamy. The mixture should leave a ribbonlike trail on the surface when lifted.

Using a large metal spoon, fold in the flour. Drizzle the melted butter over the surface, then fold it in carefully (the mixture will lose some volume).

Spoon the mixture into the prepared madeleine molds, filling each to about two-thirds full. Bake for about 10-12 minutes until lightly golden and just firm. Let cool for 1 minute, then turn out onto a wire rack to cool completely. Lightly dust with confectioners' sugar, then serve.

3 eggs

⅓ cup sugar

grated zest of 1 lemon (optional)

½ cup self-rising flour, sifted twice

5½ tablespoons unsalted butter, melted and cooled

confectioners' sugar, for dusting

18-20 madeleine molds, brushed with melted butter and dusted with sugar

Makes 18-20

chocolate truffle cake

An extra-special treat for chocaholics—made even more indulgent when served with lots of whipped cream and fresh cherries. Use good-quality chocolate for maximum flavor.

8 oz. bittersweet chocolate
¼ cup unsweetened cocoa, sifted
4 eggs, lightly beaten
½ cup confectioners' sugar, sifted, plus extra for dusting
1 tablespoon cornstarch
⅔ cup heavy cream, lightly whipped

To serve:
lightly whipped cream
fresh cherries, pitted (optional)

an 8-inch springform cake pan, greased and lined with waxed paper or parchment

Serves 6–8

Preheat the oven to 350°F. Melt the chocolate in a heatproof bowl set over a saucepan of barely simmering water (don't let the bowl touch the water). When just melted, remove from the heat and stir in the cocoa. Mix well and let cool until lukewarm.

Using an electric hand-mixer, whisk the eggs, sugar, and cornstarch until pale and doubled in volume. Using a large metal spoon, fold in the cooled chocolate, then the cream.

Pour the mixture into the prepared cake pan and bake for about 1 hour or until a toothpick inserted into the center comes out clean.

Remove from the oven and run a sharp knife around the edge of the pan. Let cool in the pan (the cake will sink a little in the middle).

Remove from the pan and dust with confectioners' sugar. To serve, cut into slices and add cream and cherries, if using.

cornish splits

"Cream teas" are comprised of splits or plain scones with clotted cream and jam, served with tea. Also known as Devonshire splits, they originated in the west of England.

Mix all the dry ingredients in a large bowl and make a well in the center. Gently heat the butter and milk in a saucepan until the butter melts. Let cool until lukewarm, then pour into the well, and mix to make a soft but not sticky dough.

Turn out onto a floured surface. Knead for 5-10 minutes until smooth and elastic. Return to the bowl, cover, and let rise at room temperature until doubled in size, about 30 minutes.

Punch down the risen dough with your knuckles, then turn out, and knead lightly. Cut into 18 pieces and shape into rolls. Set apart on the prepared baking sheets, cover, and let rise as before until doubled in size, about 20 minutes.

Preheat the oven to 425°F. Brush the rolls with milk to glaze, then bake for about 15-20 minutes until well risen and golden. Remove from the oven and let cool on a wire rack.

Lightly dust the buns with confectioners' sugar, then split them in half, and fill with cream and jam.

2½ **cups unbleached white bread flour**

1 **teaspoon sugar**

¼ **teaspoon salt**

¼ **oz. packet dry yeast**

¼ **cup unsalted butter**

1 **cup 1% milk, plus extra for brushing**

confectioners' sugar, for dusting

Filling:
1 **cup clotted cream or heavy cream, whipped**
½ **cup strawberry jam**

two baking sheets, lightly greased

Makes 18

mango scones
with *peaches and cream*

Delicious mango replaces raisins in this modern version of the classic fruit scone. I think scones are best eaten the day they're made, served with fresh fruit and cream or butter.

Preheat the oven to 400°F. Put the flour in a bowl and rub in the butter with your fingertips until the mixture looks like fine crumbs. Stir in the dried mango or papaya and sugar. Add the milk and mix to form a soft but not sticky dough.

Turn out onto a floured surface and pat out to about 1-inch thick. Dip the cookie cutter in flour and press out as many rounds as possible. Gather the trimmings, pat out again, and cut out more rounds.

Put the scones on the prepared baking sheet and brush the tops with milk. Bake for about 10-15 minutes until risen and golden. Remove from the oven and let cool on a wire rack.

To serve, split open the scones and spread each half with cream, then top with the peach slices.

1¾ cups self-rising flour, sifted
4 tablespoons unsalted butter, chilled and cut into cubes
⅓ cup chopped dried mango or papaya
2 tablespoons sugar
⅔ cup milk, plus extra for brushing

To serve:
1 cup clotted cream or heavy cream, whipped
2 ripe peaches, pitted and sliced

a 2½-inch fluted cookie cutter
a baking sheet, lightly greased

Makes 8

red tomato chutney

1 lb. ripe tomatoes, skinned and
  chopped*

1 medium onion, finely chopped

2 apples, cored and chopped

1 cup brown sugar

⅓ cup golden raisins

2 cups red wine vinegar

2 teaspoons salt

2 teaspoons ground ginger

2 tablespoons mustard seeds,
  wrapped and tied in a square
  of cheesecloth

a few drops of Tabasco or hot
  chili sauce

Fills three 16-oz. jars

***Note: Slit the skin of the tomatoes and put in
a bowl of boiling water. Let stand for 1 minute.
Drain. The skins will peel off easily.**

A fantastic accompaniment to thick wedges of cheese and crusty bread, chicken or ham sandwiches, or savory scones and muffins.

Put all the ingredients in a preserving pan or large heavy-bottom saucepan. Bring to a boil, stirring. Lower the heat and simmer, stirring often, for 30–40 minutes until reduced and slightly thickened, with a deep red color. Remove and discard the cheesecloth bag. Spoon the chutney into warm, sterilized jars and seal. Store in the refrigerator for up to 1 month.

chive and parsley butter

Herb butters add flavor to sandwiches, savory scones, and muffins. Vary the herbs—basil or dill are delicious too.

Put the butter and herbs in a bowl and beat until mixed. Transfer to a butter dish or shape into pats.

Variation:
Orange butter: for a sweet version, omit the herbs and beat in the grated zest and juice of 1 orange and 2 tablespoons confectioners' sugar.

8 tablespoons (1 stick) unsalted butter, softened
2 tablespoons snipped chives
2 tablespoons chopped parsley

Serves 6-8

apricot preserve

My favorite preserve for spooning onto freshly baked scones. Peaches are wonderful this way too. Select fruit that is ripe but not bruised.

Cut the apricots into quarters, then remove and discard the stones. Weigh the prepared fruit and for every 1 lb., weigh ½ lb. of preserving sugar.

Put the sugar, lemon juice, and 1 cup water in a large heavy-bottom saucepan. Gently heat, stirring until the sugar dissolves and the mixture is syrupy. Add the apricots, increase the heat, and boil, without stirring, for 15–20 minutes until the fruit is soft but not mushy. Remove from the heat and transfer the apricots to warm, sterilized jars with a slotted spoon.

Return the saucepan to the heat and boil the syrup for about 15 minutes or until it reaches setting point*. Pour into the jars to cover the apricots, then seal. Store in a cool place for up to 1 month.

3 lb. apricots
preserving sugar (see method)
2 tablespoons freshly squeezed
   lemon juice

Fills two 16-oz. jars

*Note: Put a teaspoon of the syrup on a plate. Chill. It is ready when a skin forms on the surface and wrinkles when a finger is pushed through it.

pink grapefruit curd

Fruit curds were a popular teatime treat in Victorian and Edwardian England. Sandwich between layers of sponge cake and scones or use as a fragrant filling for tarts and pastries.

Put the butter and sugar in a heatproof bowl set over a saucepan of simmering water (the bottom of the bowl should not touch the water). Stir until the butter melts and the sugar dissolves. Add the egg yolks, grapefruit zest, and juice. Gently heat, stirring until the mixture thickens, about 20-25 minutes.

Spoon into a warm, sterilized jar and seal. Store in the refrigerator for up to 1 month.

5½ tablespoons unsalted butter
⅔ cup sugar
3 egg yolks, lightly beaten
grated zest and juice of 1 pink
   grapefruit

Fills one 16-oz. jar

index

Page numbers in italics refer
to the illustrations.